The Child Whisperer

Matt Pasquinilli

Asian Arts Press
27 West Whipp Rd.
Dayton, Ohio 45459

D1059168

ISBN 0-9712146-0-3

First printing May 2001
Second printing April 2002

This book is dedicated to children.

Acknowledgements

Mom and Dad, for your example of unselfish love and caring. My brother Andrew, for your support and commitment. Master Choi, for your guidance and wisdom. Miss Choi, for your inspiration and uncompromising spirit. Carrie Haley, for your support and encouragement. Debbie Plasterer, Carolyn Zengel, Lou Gasaway, James Kim, Lisa Wood, David Bailey, Chris Bonnette, Tim Stanforth, Tim Boyer, Kenny Gruel, Mike Scarborough, Amy Lauck, Andy Skeen, and all the many OMAC instructors who are my brothers and sisters in this work. Master Kennedy, Master Cahn, and Master Ho Kim who have lead me through their examples of lifelong commitment and learning.

Liz Schroeder, without you, this book would not have been possible. Thank you for your friendship and faith.

Foreword

Several years ago I read a book called the Horse Whisperer. I was moved by the gentle and compassionate way in which the main character used communication to heal an abused and wild horse. A few years ago I met a man who used simple communication to help children and adults learn how to be more focused and avoid unnecessary emotional pain through discipline and self-control.

In September of 1999, I walked into a local martial arts school with my seven year old daughter, anxious to sign up for a new challenge. As we walked through the doors I was immediately overcome with a feeling of warmth. My daughter smiled brightly as she entered the class and spent an hour totally entranced by the gentle leadership of the instructor. She walked out glowing, amazed by her ability to follow and learn so quickly. The compassion that flowed so easily from the lead instructor, Matthew Pasquinilli, was inspiring.

After a month of watching my daughter grow and change through her experience in martial arts class I was increasingly anxious to further understand the philosophy that Matt obviously embraced. I set up a meeting with him so I could be educated on his teaching and talk about my daughters growing passion for the discipline. I spent two hours listening to him talk about children; his deep understanding of the human spirit intrigued me. I could hear the honesty and devotion in his voice as he spoke about his beliefs and techniques. His knowledge left me speechless. At this point, I decided that I wanted my four year-old daughter to share in this experience.

I watched my children learn the meaning of forgiveness, compassion, loyalty, dedication, the difference between discipline and self-discipline, self-control, patience and respect of parents and siblings. These were all qualities and behaviors I strive to teach in our home and it was so refreshing to have my girls hear them from someone else. I watched my children overcome challenges both physical and mental at the guidance of a gentle soul. I watched gifted children gain confidence in social situations. I watched abused foster children learn to smile and communicate. I watched children begin the program running wildly through the school slowly learn to focus and concentrate with ease. And I also watched parents learn to be better parents, including myself.

Matt's devotion to his students is powerful. He understands the true meaning of the individual and treats each student with equal respect. He believes fully in each student and enables him or her to make constant progresses and feel constant growth. His persistence in constant growth and change in himself allows him to be an extraordinary leader and teacher. His patience and compassion is ever present. His deep and natural understanding of human nature at its core allows him to speak to the soul, to touch the heart and to reach the child in everyone. His

communication is like a whisper, the child whisperer.

Liz Schroeder

Table of Contents

Introduction

Chapter 1 Building Confidence

Chapter 2 Focus

Chapter 3 Communication

Chapter 4 Self-Regulation

Chapter 5 Respect

Chapter 6 Leadership

Chapter 7 Success

Chapter 8 Forgiveness

Chapter 9 Truth and Honesty

Chapter 10 Community

Chapter 11 Vision

Introduction

How we communicate with our children will determine what kind of adults they will grow up to be. Communication is often taken for granted, and how we communicate is not something we think about while we are doing it. The methods in this book have been learned by watching how children react to the language we adults use to communicate with them.

Each chapter contains a few paragraphs defining the concept and method needed to improve communication. I intentionally wrote very brief descriptions so that the reader is not drowned in language, and can quickly understand the main points of the concept and method.

After the method has been introduced, I share an anecdote from my experience working with children. The anecdote should be helpful in illustrating how the method can be applied. In some chapters, I also list some tools that can be used to apply the method in a very simple way.

Because confidence and esteem affects how you communicate, the book begins the journey of learning effective communication skills with some truths about confidence, and how it can be improved.

The second chapter talks about the skill of focus. I call focus a skill, because we all have the ability to focus, but getting children to focus on the right thing at the right time will improve their performance in school, and aid their ability to communicate and listen to adults.

Chapter three describes how we speak to others affects the way we speak to ourselves. The information in this chapter should be used to help discern the patterns of communication our children use, and how changing those patterns can empower them to make positive change in their lives.

The concept of self-regulation is introduced in chapter four as a device your child can use to avoid getting in trouble for making the mistakes or breaches of good judgment. Self-regulation is a popular concept in psychology, and the method described in chapter four is a simple approach to its application.

A respectful child is well liked by the adults in his or her life. I chapter five I define what respect should look like in the behavior of a child, and how defining respect for children allows them to take ownership of it.

Chapter six is about leadership by example. Teaching and raising children requires that you demonstrate all of the character traits and skills you want your child to have. Leadership, as described in this book, asks you to take a look at yourself and check your own behavior for signs of what your child might be mirroring.

In chapter seven I define success, as I understand it. In the United States and many Western countries, success has been defined as achieving a goal that you have set for yourself. I understand success to be more about the journey than the destination. The definition of success in chapter seven is recognition of progress.

Forgiveness of our own shortcomings and failures is the key to happiness. Chapter eight urges you to let go of your mistakes, and see them for what they really are. Making a mistake is part of being human, and if you strive to be perfect, you are denying your own humanity. Additionally, if you cannot demonstrate self-forgiveness in front of your children, then they will model their behavior on yours.

In chapter nine I attempt to define truth and honesty. Understanding and knowing truth is a path that we must take, and a destination we may never reach because of our humanity. We can work toward understanding truth by living as honestly as possible, but we have to be prepared to forgive ourselves when we leave the path from time to time.

All of these concepts and methods do not work unless applied in community with others. Chapter ten describes the value of community, and how we can structure a community that supports our children and ourselves.

I conclude the book by describing my vision of the application of these techniques and methods to our society. Our society moves in mega trends, which are hard to see while we are moving within them. With our effort, we can provide our children a life of less pain and emotional suffering.

Chapter 1 Building Confidence

Confidence comes from proof of our ability to do something. This ability is the application of a skill we have developed through practice. The skill we have practiced was learned by us after we opened our minds to the possibility of our being able to develop the skill. This opening of our mind came after we broke free from whatever belief may have been there before. This breaking of the old belief is a form of physical and emotional housecleaning.

The first step to build confidence is cleansing. Our body cleans itself out by sweating, breathing, elimination (going to the bathroom), and shedding skin. We aid this cleansing through vigorous and regular exercise. Emotional cleansing is also aided by physical exercise, which releases chemicals that balance adrenalin. Better respiration aids emotional cleansing by richly oxygenating the blood flowing into the brain.

After we have cleansed our body and mind, we must learn new ways to think, speak, and act. Using exercise, we can train our bodies to respond to stress by breathing deeply, developing correct posture, and creating an ability to make and maintain eye contact. By finding new and more positive ways in which to see ourselves, and the roles we play in this life, we can learn new methods and techniques to improve our emotional health and self-image.

In order for these techniques and methods to become skills, we must practice them consistently and diligently. This training is a conditioning at a very fundamental level. For example, the cells in our body do not know the difference between physical and emotional stress. This means that we can condition our body to breathe in response to great physical stress from running or other similar exercise, so that when we experience an equivalent amount of emotional stress, the body naturally begins to breathe and our stress will be reduced.

After a skill has been developed, it must be applied to acquire proof of success. If a child has been trained to focus on schoolwork, and through application, receives grades better than ever before, the proof is the improved report card. By conditioning her body to handle stress with breathing, proof of success might be recognition by an employer of calmness under pressure. The result could be a promotion or monetary bonus.

One boy jumped 38 points in IQ

Using the four steps of building confidence, we designed a program that combined a sophisticated system of martial arts movements with a unique teaching method. The purpose of the program was to help children and adults to change the way they felt about themselves in order to cause positive social change.

A local psychotherapist referred a group of low income and foster children to our program. All of the children had experienced some form of physical, emotional, or sexual abuse. Many of these children scored very low on their intelligence tests, and the psychotherapist attributed their poor performance to the children's inability to overcome feelings of low self-worth and depressed self-esteem. She thought that these children might be able to improve their test scores if they were able to better handle the stress they felt from the challenge of the timed IQ test.

All of the children in the program seemed average in intelligence, but their scores defined them as mentally deficient. When giving the IQ test the first time, the proctor of the test recorded their comments and body language. Some of them would say things like, "I'm just too stupid to do this." or run from the table and refuse to continue. We saw them as products of their upbringing, and thought that we could break their patterns of behavior, which were keeping them from scoring accurately.

Applying the first step of cleansing was a challenge because it required a lot of pushing them past their levels of comfort. This means that they would cry, threaten the teacher, yell at the teacher, and use inappropriate body language to show their emotions. Consistency paid off though, and after six weeks, the children were able to break their conditioned behavior through vigorous exercise, which caused them to sweat and breathe more deeply and completely. This prepared them for the next step.

After they were able to consistently break through their old behavior and let go of emotions of inferiority, the students were then taught to handle their stress by slowing down their breathing and using the focusing skills described in the next chapter. This gave them a way to handle the stress of the test, but the techniques now had to be practiced enough to become natural to their bodies.

Training of these new techniques consisted of lots of running and other vigorous exercise, and then stopping and forcing control of breathing and the motion of the body. This step is monotonous and can be boring for the child. We use praise and positive recognition to encourage our students, and not punishment. This positive approach to leading the children to develop self-discipline in training allowed them to harden their techniques until they became skills. The final step was application.

In the martial arts, we use board breaking to give proof of success to the student when they apply a physical technique. In order to prove to the students that their new techniques of breathing and focus could work when applied to the test, we would ask them to apply these skills whenever faced with emotional challenges. Using a parent report card and teacher evaluation form, we chose one or more inappropriate behaviors for each child, and gave the child a short period of time in which to change these behaviors using their new skills. One boy would hit his sister whenever he got angry, and so we asked him to apply his breathing and physical control to release and manage his anger whenever he recognized he was getting upset. Another three-year-old girl was preparing to testify in court against the men who had raped her, and we asked her to use the breathing and eye contact to control her fear and speak out against her assailants. As the children were successful, and had proof of their success through their accomplishments, their confidence grew.

When the second intelligence tests were administered, all children who had consistent participation in the program made marked improvement. One boy jumped thirty-eight points, moving himself up from learning disabled classes at school to regular classes.

Four Steps of Building Confidence / Causing Behavior to Change

Cleansing

> sweating
>
> respiration
>
> digestive waste elimination
>
> emotional release

Learning – introduction of skills needed to change behavior and become successful

> new ways of handling stress
>
> > 3 deep slow breaths
> >
> > correct posture
> >
> > physical self-control
> >
> > forced smiling
>
> new beliefs and information (as described in later chapters)

how to focus

eye contact

body control

mental concentration

appropriate communication

non-emotional language

speaking honestly and truthfully

giving information instead of making
accusations

definitions of respect according to each
specific relationship

Training – hardening of skills

practice or repetition of techniques
learned

conditioning of the body through
exercise

Application – with self-grading (as described in later
chapters)

skills learned and trained now become
abilities

proof of success

success is defined as recognition of progress

three questions of self-regulation

> "where am I?" – determines what the
> rules will be

> "what am I supposed to be doing" –
> defines the rules which must be
> followed

> "what am I doing" – are the rules being
> followed?

five point self-grading system

> give one point for doing what you are
> supposed to

> second point is for eye contact

> third point is for body control

> fourth point is for mental concentration

> fifth point is for breathing in order to
> remain focused

Chapter 2 Focus

When considering our ability to pay attention
to what we are doing, we usually think in terms of
focus. Incorrectly, we might think that we are not
able to focus if we are easily distractible. The truth is
that we are focused on something other than the thing
we wish to focus on. If a child's report card reads,
"unfocused", or "lacks concentration", then this
definition of what focus is should be helpful in
creating a solution.

There are three basic areas of focus or
concentration. The first is eye focus, or eye contact.
Children who may be diagnosed with Attention
Deficit Disorder (ADD), or Attention Deficit
Hyperactivity Disorder (ADHD) very often will not
be able to naturally maintain eye contact for long
periods of time. A highly distractible person is
sometimes defined as someone who looks around the

room non-stop, one who looks at everything and is not content in looking at any one thing for very long. Training this person to focus their eyes on the person or thing they need to attend to is the first step in increasing their attention span.

The second area of concentration is body control, or body focus. It is necessary for us to move our bodies in order to be healthy human beings. Some boys and girls have more of a need to move their bodies more frequently than others, and will stand out in a class of other children who do not move around nearly as much. No matter what the reason for their need to move, these extra-active children can be trained to control their bodies by releasing the stress that builds from inactivity. Breathing is a natural way to relieve the need to move the body, and so can be learned and practiced by an active child.

After the child has developed eye contact and body control, mental focus should be taught and trained. Mental focus is a basic mindfulness, or the child thinking about what he or she is doing, hearing, or saying. Self-regulation is the tool used to develop and apply this skill. Proper response to a parent or teacher, such as, "yes mom", "yes "Mrs. Teacher", is an appropriate measure of how well the child is focusing on what they are being told by the adult. Training the child to repeat some of what has been told to them may be necessary when working with a highly distractible child. It is important to remember that mental focus will be misplaced if the child is not looking at the adult or their work, and if parts of their body are in constant and rapid motion (fidgeting.)

In order to maintain focus and increase the attention span, have the child apply slow and deep breathing to relieve the stress built up from the difficulty of making eye contact, standing or sitting still, and mental challenges like boredom or emotional discomfort. When we breathe, the lungs fill with air, straightening the back and oxygenating the blood. Because it is difficult to breath deeply when the head is moving around, a deep breath will bring the head, and therefore the eyes, upright and to the front. Oxygen in the blood relaxes fidgeting muscles and aids in calming the muscles. Mental focus is improved when the oxygen rich blood reaches and refreshes the brain. Three deep and slow breaths is the rule, and should be encouraged before a conversation with a child is even begun.

In five minutes a five-year-old boy was able to learn simple multiplication.

In between classes I make time to talk to children who are under-performing in school. I like to ask questions that let them assess their own ability. One boy was getting in trouble for his behavior at school. His kindergarten teacher had sent a note home to his mom telling of how he had wetted his hair in the bathroom and made a mess on the floor with the water.

I asked the boy why he had gone to the bathroom in the first place, and he said that he didn't like class because he was too stupid to do the class work. We talked about how he could use his skills of focus to improve his ability to learn and understand the things he was being taught. As an example, I asked him if he would learn multiplication for me.

After explaining what multiplication is, I gave him three simple rules that he had to apply in order to multiply two numbers. The multiplication rules are simple and universal, but the key to his success would be his ability to stay focused long enough to remember them and apply them.

While describing the multiplication method, I reminded him to look at me, sit still, and think about what I was saying. After five minutes, I gave him a paper of fifteen problems to solve. He finished them quickly, and then came up with his own multiplication problems to solve. He took the problems home as his proof of success, and has excelled in class ever since.

Tools you can use with your child to improve their ability to focus

Eye contact.

When talking with your child, require eye contact first. If in the middle of your talk, your child looks away from your eyes, start over from the beginning after reminding him to look at your eyes. Do this as often as necessary until eye contact is consistent.

During class work or homework, eye contact becomes looking at the paper or thing the child is working on. While riding a bike, eye contact is looking at the road. Speaking to someone requires that the eyes make visual contact with the eyes of the person you are talking to.

Body control.

After your child is able to look at you, then tell him to stand or sit still. Stop and start over as often as necessary until the body is still during the whole conversation.

During class work or homework, body control is sitting still with correct posture - a good chair and uncluttered working surface will aid body control. While riding a bike, body control is good posture with correct movement of the body to cause forward movement. Speaking to someone requires that the body remains still so that the person who you are talking to is not distracted.

Of course you should not be stiff and unanimated while talking to someone, but children sometimes twist their torsos and swing their arms while talking to an adult, or might stick their fingers in their mouths or place their hands over their entire face. This might be a sign of being emotionally uncomfortable, but it can be distracting to both the child and the adult. Self-control of the body during a conversation helps a child overcome an inability to express himself verbally due to emotional distress. The physical movement is like an emotional pressure release valve – simply replace that form of pressure release with deep breathing, and the child will be able to say what they need to.

Mental focus.

Ask the child to respond with "yes Mom", or "yes Dad", when you have finished telling them something. If a child tends to forget easily, then ask them to repeat the main points of what you have told them. Do this consistently until you are satisfied that "yes Mom", or "yes Dad", is sufficient.

During class work or homework, mental focus becomes thinking about the assignment while the child is working on it. While riding a bike, mental focus is thinking about traffic, the surface they are riding on, where they are going, etc. Speaking to someone requires that the child think about what they say before they say it, and that the child thinks about what they are being told.

Children often get into trouble for reacting to their emotions by saying things that are intended to ease their emotional suffering in one of two ways. First, they might yell or scream something mean like, "I don't care" or "I hate you." Lying or concealing the truth is the other way children might react to an emotional confrontation. Ask your child to take three deep breaths before they speak in order to give them time to think about their response so that they might avoid saying something they might regret.

Chapter 3 Communication

Communication is the key to a successful relationship, and how we speak to others is how we speak to ourselves. To have good emotional health, we must be able to speak honestly and openly about how we feel, what upsets us, and how we see ourselves.

When we become upset with ourselves, we experience emotional pain. Our subconscious tendency is to run from this pain in order to lessen it. Some examples of ways in which children communicate when upset are baby talk, whining, rapid speech with animated body language, low or soft voice while looking at the ground, the use of a loud, aggressive voice with angry body language, and steadfastly refusing to speak.

Children learn to use communication by following a model presented by their parents. When a child is yelled at, they tend to yell, when a parent uses baby talk to lessen the stress of a disappointed or upset child, then the child will likely use baby talk when stressed. Children are often said to be the mirror of the parent, and how a child communicates often presents the clearest image of how the adult communicates.

Repeating inappropriate behavior and mistakes.

The need for straightforward and honest communication in children is demonstrated when a child repeats a mistake or inappropriate behavior over a long period of time. Saying "sorry" often relieves the emotional stress we feel because of our guilt. If I dismiss this guilt too quickly, I may not be able to fully understand what I did, and how I can avoid doing the same thing in the future.

When working with a child who repeats the same mistake or unwanted behavior, you can interrupt their apology and redirect her back to her guilt. Saying, "don't say 'sorry', just don't do it again" is an example of how you might redirect a child back to a more mindful state which can allow them to make a conscious effort to change a behavior.

Inability to communicate needs and wants.

When we are unable to voice what we need or want, negative emotions build and stack upon each other, ultimately ruining our relationships. If someone says or does something that hurts or disturbs us, and we can't express ourselves in a way that empowers us to have control over our own emotions, we can eventually break the relationship.

Children who do not speak when upset or experiencing guilt are avoiding emotional pain. Using breathing as a technique allows them to reduce emotional pressure, and eye contact opens a channel for them to begin communicating.

Inappropriate emotional relationships

During martial arts class, we sometimes wear protective padding so that we may hit each other with controlled kicks and punches. While the whole concept of hitting another person for any reason is controversial, it is a vital component of most martial arts training. We use it to teach control, divide physical pain from emotional pain, and to teach communication.

As students practice their techniques with a partner, the instructors constantly monitor their actions and behavior. A student who is getting hit too hard by their partner is taught to say, "You hit me too hard." Their partner must then say, "Ok." That is all. Saying sorry is too easy, and the next time they hit their partner, they must simply hit with more control. If more control is exercised, and the hit is not too hard, then the partner must say, "That was not too hard." This gives recognition of the offending partner's change of behavior. The instructor is physically present to enforce control if the student does not use self-control (after being told that the hit is too hard).

Without this method of communication, the students may develop a negative emotional relationship. The true relationship between the two students is based on a simple practical need. One student delivers the hit and the other receives it. Any emotions shared between the two are not appropriate in this relationship. The teacher to student relationship should be based on the same practical need.

The student-to-teacher relationship is simple. The teacher delivers the material and the student receives it. In our class, a hard working student may be paired with a student who is unfocused or playing around. If one student is trying to work hard, and the other student's behavior does not allow it, an emotional relationship may develop. The hard working student begins to despise the unfocused student but does not say anything. In this situation, we train the student to say, "Stop playing", or, "Look at me", or "Stand still." A teacher should also use this simple form of communication in order to avoid developing an emotional relationship with a student who displays disrespectful behavior.

Conflict resolution on the playground

"It hurts my feelings when you hit me." Or "I don't like it when you call me stupid." These are very common ways in which children are urged to confront other children when assaulted physically or verbally. This language is a form of rejection on an emotional level, and often causes the opposite of the desired outcome to happen. The guilty child is not able to feel guilt, because he is feeling rejected and must defend himself by arguing, lying about his action, or plotting some revenge for a later time. The child who was assaulted lingers in his own rejection by using the language of emotion to confront his assailant, and is thus hurt by maintaining an inappropriate emotional relationship with the other child.

A more healthy approach is for the child who has been harmed to confront his assailant with clear and emotionless language. He might say, "Don't hit me." or "Don't say those things to me." Using this method, he simply communicates his need for the other child to not assault him. An adult is present so that the other child might realize that a consequence to his action or continued action may be imminent if he continues to assault his victim.

Jealousy and competition between children cause a lot of inappropriate emotional relationships to develop, and the laissez faire environment found on many playgrounds allows arguments, shouting matches, and physical confrontations, which can impair a child's ability to stay focused when the child returns to class. Conflict resolution on the playground requires honest and straightforward communication.

Giving information is the key to successfully diffusing a playground conflict. Expressing emotion by saying that, "It hurt my feelings when you ..." assumes that the action was intentional, and passes judgment on the behavior of the offending child. While it might seem obvious to a teacher that a child's action was intended to physically or emotionally harm another child, true resolution of the conflict can only be had by reserving judgment until all information is discovered by both sides. This discovery happens when both children are giving and asking for information.

Statements that create inappropriate emotional relationships between children:

"It hurt my feelings when you…"

"I don't like it when you…"

"Can you please not?"

Statements that give or ask for information in order to avoid an inappropriate emotional relationship:

"You did …"

"Why did you ..?"

"Are you angry with me?"

"Don't … to me again."

You may use this same technique with siblings who fight at home.

Chapter 4 Self-Regulation

We do not choose to be embarrassed or ridiculed for our mistakes. Children do not choose to be punished for their actions either. Consequences of our poor judgment must be experienced in order for us to learn the parameters of acceptable social behavior, and in order for us to not repeat the same mistakes; we must regulate our behavior by through the application of three questions.

The first thing we need to know is where we are. Where we are will determine the socially acceptable set of behaviors we must not breach in order to exist in harmony with our environment and our neighbors. When a child is in school, the set of rules he must follow is different than the set he must follow at home. Even during the school day, he has different rules at recess than he does in the classroom.

After we make ourselves aware of where we are, we must know the rules that define appropriate behavior. If a child knows what they are supposed to be doing, then they can chose to follow the rules or break them. Very few children will intentionally break the rules. Once we are mindful of what we are supposed to be doing, we must then check to see whether or not we are doing it.

If a child is doing what he or she is supposed to, then that child will not be punished. When a child regulates his or her own behavior, then the child has chosen to exercise self-discipline.

The difference between discipline and self-discipline

Discipline is following the rules, and the language of discipline is often harsh and unwelcome. To a child it sounds like this: "Stop talking and sit in your seat." or "Look at me when I am talking to you." No one likes being told what to do, especially children.

Self-Discipline is applying the rules without being told to, and is the language of praise and recognition. It sounds like this "Joey is sitting quietly in his seat" or "Thank you for making eye contact with me when I talk to you." We thrive on recognition and praise.

Using self-regulation, a child is able to choose the praise and recognition of self-discipline over the harsh language of discipline. Adults enjoy praise and recognition as much as children, and self-regulation in adult behavior allows adults to challenge and overcome their weaknesses of character and habit.

No one chooses to be punished for making a mistake.

I once overheard a teacher telling a boy that he chose to be punished by choosing not to control himself. This teacher was reinforcing a negative behavior, and she was mistaken in assuming that he made a decision to do the wrong thing.

Making a decision to act in some way implies that we are thinking about what we are doing. Many adults do not possess the level of mental presence required to consistently take intentional action. It is wrong to assume that a child acts with a mindfulness of purpose without first being trained to do so. The greatest success of our program comes in this area of training.

During our "Summer of Success" summer day camp program, we teach the children to check their behavior by first asking three simple questions. The first is, "Where am I?" The answer to this question will allow the child to know what the rules might be.

The second question is "What am I supposed to be doing?" This is another way of asking, "What are the rules I should be following?" After the child knows *what* he should be doing, he needs to ask, "What *am* I doing?" If he is doing anything other than what he is supposed to, then he simply changes his behavior positively.

Using this method, we had great success (with rapid change) in the children's behavior at home. The proof of their success gave them confidence to apply this method at school. Several children who had not been meeting performance expectations at school the previous year were able to make dramatic improvements in their grades at school after participation in the summer day camp program.

Five-point grading system

After the child is consistently checking his or her behavior, we move on to a five- point grading system. This system allows them to better define the quality of what they are doing, and to reward themselves for doing well. It is important to move on to this step so that the adult does not need to constantly check the child's performance.

Taking one physical skill, we define it in five ways. For example, standing at attention is one way that we train the student to develop physical control. The first point in the system will always be for doing what you are supposed to be doing. After that, we give one point for eye contact, one point for standing still, one point for thinking about what you are doing, and the last point for deep and slow breathing. If a child is doing all five, then she has the most points possible; if not, then she simply changes her behavior in order to earn her points. This is very simple and children respond to it very well.

After children are rewarding themselves with five points consistently, then you should add points for other things that better define the task they are required to perform.

Check yourself before it is too late

When working with children, I use the following scenarios to illustrate the need for self-regulation.

When you get grounded from watching television or playing with your friends because your grades are bad, then it is too late to change your grades. If you are checking yourself while you are in school, then you will know when you are not doing well, and be able to change to doing the right thing.

When you see the tear rolling down your mother's face because you just yelled, "I hate you." Then it is too late to take back what you said no matter how bad you feel. If you are checking your behavior, then you will know that you are not breathing to control your temper, and you can start breathing before it is too late.

Chapter 5 Respect

Respect is widely used when talking about issues that confront our self- esteem. Human beings have a basic need to be accepted by the rest of humanity. When rejected by a friend, a lover, a child, or even a stranger, we feel attacked in the center of our being.

Recognizing that disrespect is a form of rejection allows us to isolate our emotion from the reality of the action or words of the person who has shown us disrespect. By doing so, we will then be able to communicate our needs and wants to that person in order to determine whether or not their action or words were really meant to reject us. This is an important skill to teach a child who is easily angered by the words or actions of his or her peers at school, or siblings at home.

A child can be taught to control their emotions by using deep and slow breaths, focusing techniques, and other physical and mental tools described in this book. When a child complains that they feel disliked and unwanted by friends at school or by brothers and sisters at home, then the child can be encouraged to talk to the other child or children about what has happened without the use of emotional language.

Showing respect to parents and teachers

If a parent is to feel respected by their child, that child must apply three skills with consistency. The first skill is attention, which consists of eye contact, body control, and mental focus. The second skill a child must apply in order for the parent to feel respected, is doing what the parent tells the child to do. The last skill a child must apply is completion of his or her own work. This means keeping their room clean, their body hair, and teeth clean, preparing for and going to bed on time, etc…

Teachers will feel respected when the child applies the same set of rules in the classroom. Focusing on the teacher during lessons, following the rules of the class, and doing their class and homework. Because teachers and parents may not always be consistently modeling respectful language and behavior for the child to follow, training the child with these three skills will allow them to consistently apply respect, and the result may be that the adult no longer feels stress from the relationship with the child. It is sometimes this stress that triggers the adult's negative response to the behavior of the child, causing the child to be exposed to inappropriate language and behavior.

Defining Respect

In order to improve your relationship with your child, help him or her to understand a very simple set of rules that need to be followed in order for you to feel respected. You can use the ones listed above, or you can come up with your own.

Look at your relationships with your spouse, friends, coworkers, boss, employees, etc… Define respect in each one of these relationships by asking yourself what you need to experience in order to feel respected. After you get comfortable with this exercise, walk your child through the same process with all of his or her relationships. If you have more than one child, this exercise is especially valuable, because it can be used to define the relationship between your children in a way that will help them see why they might fight and tell on each other so much.

Chapter 6 Leadership

One truth about children is that they are the product of their upbringing. They are a reflection of the adults who are raising them. An abused child grows to abuse children. A well-loved child grows to love children. Leadership is the act of being the human being we wish others to be by modeling that behavior for them.

Mahatma Gandhi said, "We must be the change we wish to see." This is the essence of leadership. How can a teacher expect a child to apply respect in the student-teacher relationship if the teacher does not apply respect to the student?

Modeling appropriate behavior is the most powerful tool we have to shape our children. If our music describes sexual acts, our movies depict gratuitous violence, we eat to excess, and we work only for material gain, then what can we expect from our children? They will act out what we live, and they will do it better and faster than we can. That is the nature of youth.

In order to discipline our children, we must first discipline ourselves. Self-regulation is the key to exercising this discipline, and where we lead, our children will follow. All that we want for our children we must first obtain for ourselves.

Leadership is a tool of empowerment for teens

Children want to be good. That is true for all human beings. Unfortunately, our popular culture glorifies all that makes us bad. Teens are voracious consumers of a corrupted media that seems bent on the destruction of all that is good and true.

Using teens as assistant instructors in our program provides an opportunity for teens to be good for the sake of their juniors. This creates in them a sense of purpose and mission, which replaces the confusion and uncertainty of the process of maturing into adults.

The young children look up to our teens, and any inappropriate action or word can break the trust of the children. We teach the teens to be aware of the awesome responsibility of leadership through example. It only works if we adults model for the teens what we expect them to be to the younger children.

The power of demonstrating emotional self-control, or leading others by example

In 1998 I took a sabbatical from teaching the martial arts to explore how other martial arts programs were defining leadership. I traveled around the country for seven months and visited more than one hundred different martial arts schools. To get quick money for travel, I worked as a restaurant waiter in some of the cities I visited.

In Atlanta, I worked at one restaurant for a time period of about three months. The environment at this restaurant was very chaotic, with very young management and typical wait staff – both young and immature, or older single mothers struggling to survive on little money. It was a great place to apply honesty in relationships.

Every waiter or waitress will have to serve unappreciative customers from time to time. Either the customers are rude and offensive, or they tip poorly or not at all. When working as a waiter or waitress, it is easy to feel rejected by an unappreciative customer, and every night I worked at the restaurant, I saw the emotional reactions demonstrated by the other wait staff to those feelings of rejection.

After a couple of weeks, some of the other wait staff asked me why it didn't seem to bother me when I was treated poorly by a customer. I told them that I could only feel rejected by the customer if I had some expectation of acceptance from that person. Their bad behavior was just bad behavior. There could be a lot of reasons why they didn't tip me well, including that they might be upset with me, but that I would only feel rejected if I expected their praise and acknowledgement. When a customer was rude or said inappropriate things, then I took three slow and deep breaths and forced a smile on my face to control and relieve my stronger feelings of rejection that were starting to build. If the customer's comment was abusive to me, I told him not to speak to me in such a way. I used an emotionless tone of voice to communicate with an abusive customer, and told him what I expected to hear in place of the abusive comments. The other wait staff were interested in learning how to develop and use the same techniques, and in a little while, they started to practice them at home and at work – when they remembered to. After a few weeks, they were reporting their successes and asking for help with understanding what they were doing wrong when a technique they were using did not always work.

After two months, most of the wait staff and some of the young managers were applying simple tools of emotional self-control and using clear communication. The restaurant became a far more peaceful place to work, and their high employee turnover rate dropped dramatically. At this point I realized that if I can train others in this method of emotional self-control and simple and straightforward communication, they could influence their family, friends, and peers. If enough of us use these techniques, then all of society begins to change. This revelation forced me to return immediately to teaching the martial arts.

Chapter 7 Success

The definition of success

Success is the recognition of progress. Commonly, success is thought of as goal setting and goal reaching. No matter how much you acquire or reach, you will be unsatisfied with yourself if you are not able to recognize your progress in whatever is important to you.

Imagine climbing a mountain. If you keep looking up, you will be daunted by how far you have not yet gone. The top of the mountain seems unreachable, and the emotional stress fatigues you greater than the physical stress of the climb itself. Look behind you and see where you have come from, and you will be constantly fueled by the proof of your progress - the base of the mountain shrinking in the distance. Before long, you have reached the top of the mountain, and are preparing for your next climb.

If we are mindful of our progress, then we always have with us the knowledge of our ability to overcome challenge through the application of skills we have learned and practiced for the challenges we face.

A child who defines her progress by whether or not she has made all A's on a report card must be helped to understand that success is measured in what she has achieved, and not what she has not. Striving to improve should always be encouraged, but attaining the goal must not be the measure.

The measure of success

Materially, we have three basic needs, which must be met if we are to survive. The first is food, the second is shelter, and the third is clothing. If we eat too much we get fat and our heart and lungs struggle to support our excess. When our shelter is excessive, we spend a lot of time and money cleaning and repairing it. Too much clothing causes others to envy us, is expensive to clean and maintain, and can give us a false image of our self. In America and the West, material success was achieved for the majority of people long ago, though we still seem attached to the notion that what you own defines your worth.

The true measure of your worth lies in the truth you live in your life. Honesty in thought, speech, and action are the measure of your success. This truth is seen in the kindness you show to others, the generosity of your actions and words, the discipline you exercise in relationships with others and with yourself. The many ways in which we are called upon to be honest do not need to be defined here. You know what these things are; whether or not you are a successful person is demonstrated through the progress you make toward improving yourself in order to live honestly.

Excerpts of a letter from a parent

"My son, age 8, has really come a long way since joining your program. Because of his Asperger's Syndrome, a form of autism, when we first walked in, his posture was poor. He looked at the floor as he walked because he didn't have the concept of his body in space. My son is now walking with his head upright and his posture is significantly changed for the better. Additionally, my son's muscle tone was very weak and he very rarely wanted to participate in anything physical because he couldn't compete with other children. His training has given him the ability to work at his own pace and therefore he no longer has a fear of losing against other children.

"My son has come ahead light years in his emotional stability. When we first joined, anything that was difficult for him, either physically or emotionally, would cause him to cry and roll on the floor. With your program's guidance and counseling, my son is now able to better process events, and no longer "throws tantrums" when things don't go his way. He is getting along better with his peers now because he is able to control his emotional outbursts. My son actually has friends now, something he did not have before because other children did not understand his emotional problems.

"His performance in school is also significantly improved. His emotional shutdowns are now a thing of the past and he is better able to talk to his teachers and explain to them what is bothering him. As a result, a solution can now be reached which allows him to continue to make progress in his education. I know that his new attitude will make this school year much easier for him, his teachers, and me.

The boy described in this letter participated in our "Summer of Success" day camp program. He came every day for about eight hours a day. He cried and rolled on the floor for the first six weeks. He was a great challenge.

His progress was very slow, but constant. By seeking progress, while working without any goal or expectation, we were able to keep sight of how he was changing, and not get stuck on how he wasn't changing. As this student moved from one level to the next, the instructors helped him to see and measure his progress. By the end of the summer, he would no longer cry or refuse to participate. For the last few weeks, he became very happy and had a pleasant manner.

Two things made this change possible. The first was the simple and consistent approach to causing behavior change – as described in this book. The second was the ability of the instructors to work with this child without developing any emotional relationship with him.

Chapter 8 Forgiveness

If you want to have great success in your life, then you must expect to make a lot of mistakes. In order to survive the guilt from these mistakes, you must learn to forgive yourself. Additionally, if you cannot forgive yourself, you will never be able to fully forgive others, and all of your relationships will break or suffer great distress.

Forgiveness is the message of many of our religions. When we think of forgiveness, we very often think of forgiveness of others and not ourselves. The truth is that we will suffer the greatest harm from our own actions and our own words. We will beat ourselves up far more viscously than anyone else ever can.

In order to forgive, we must see our emotions for what they really are. A creation of our mind, our emotions are products of a set of beliefs about how we are and how we should be. No one of us strives to be mean, but at times we are mean. We don't want to overindulge, but at times we do. In some Christian faiths, the Ten Commandments are seen as a list of how every one of us are, the absolution of our souls by the death of Christ is seen by some Christians as the forgiveness of our human nature, and a message that we cannot progress in our humanity until we forgive ourselves. The key to obtaining enlightenment and happiness in many religious beliefs is the acceptance of our humanity. A famous Buddhist koan, (or question asked in order to guide a follower toward enlightenment), asks, "Who was I before I was born, who am I after I am gone, who am I now?" To answer this question, the student must first confront his or her humanity.

Refusing to forgive ourselves is a defense mechanism that we use to avoid the emotional pain of guilt. By avoiding this guilt, we are destined to repeat the same mistakes. In order to face our weakness, we must accept that we are weak and live in the pain of guilt. Knowing how we are is the first step to forgiving ourselves for being human.

Pride is the enemy of forgiveness, and forces us to reject our humanity. We place ourselves above human frailty by refusing to acknowledge our weaknesses. Lowering yourself and bowing before the truth of being human is very difficult because of the pain of failure. Many men and women experience great success in their lives after a great awakening. The awakening is always precipitated by some great failure, which cannot be overcome by pride.

As children we were encouraged to strive toward independence as defined by self-determination. The adults in our lives modeled behavior, which taught us that we could control our own destiny if we only work hard enough. The phrase, "You can do anything if you put your mind to it." has misguided many of us to believe that we need only to work harder in order to avoid all mistakes and reach the highest level of attainment and achievement. But success is recognition of our progress, and we cannot make progress if we avoid knowing how we are.

It's not who you are, but how you are that matters

We are encouraged to know ourselves by defining who we are. This is misguided, because the definition of who we are is tied into knowing the truth of how we are. So first, set out to know how you are.

Some good clues to how you are will be evident in how you react to others. The weakness of others might really anger you, and there is an answer to the question of how you are. Prejudice is born of self-hate. Examine what you hate most about the people you despise, and then examine yourself closely.

Let go of your shortcomings

Your mistakes are proof that you are alive and making progress. The older we get, the harder it is to forgive ourselves for being imperfect. Children learn to beat themselves up over their failure by watching us strive to be perfect. We need to model humanity for our children by accepting and forgiving our shortcomings when they arise.

Learning forgiveness changed my life

This work is very hard and emotionally draining at times. The most difficult thing about my job is the constant assessment of my personal behavior, and as a result, constantly seeing my shortcomings. The greatest danger comes when we lose sight of our humanity, and deny our weaknesses.

In the fifth year of doing this work, I told a child to shut up. It was a major breach of self-control, and I was devastated. I wrote a letter of resignation and prepared to quit this work for good. Because I had expected myself to be perfect, I was shocked when I fell short.

My instructor is a very wise and gifted man. He refused to let me quit and called me arrogant and proud. I was shocked and offended. I thought that of all the things I was, arrogant was not one of them. My life had been dedicated to serving others through the martial arts. I made less than ten thousand dollars a year and slept on the floor of the martial arts school. How could I be proud and arrogant if I were so giving of myself to other people? His answer changed my life.

"Your success is written on the face of every child you teach. You can't see that because you are focused on your one tiny mistake." Wow! The power of that observation allowed me to forgive myself and accept my failure for what it was. My instructor had turned me around so that I could see where I had come from, instead of focusing on where I had not yet gone.

(A martial arts master is someone who has a demonstrated mastery of physical techniques and philosophy, not someone who has mastership over another person.)

Chapter 9 Truth and Honesty

Truth is defined by the nature of our being. Honesty defines the laws of that nature, and is the journey we must take in order to understand truth. Honesty defines how you are, and knowledge of how you are will guide you toward knowing who and what you are.

At the root of all human suffering is the division of man from truth. As a result of our separation from truth, the capacity of human understanding requires the use of a vocabulary that divides all our experiences into two categories – good and bad.

Emotions do not exist in the nature of the universe; they are necessary only for our survival outside of it. Human will challenges the law of nature by trying to control it. Emotions are contrary to honesty, and so the key to living honestly is learning how to control our emotions.

When something happens to us that meets our expectations in a welcomed way, then we understand that event as good. When the un-welcomed occurs, then it feels bad to us. The nature of our existence cannot be defined as consisting of good and bad, but instead, the nature of our existence must be defined as simply *being*.

If a child is running on the sidewalk and falls, he might receive a cut on his knee. The physical pain comes and goes quickly, but the fear caused by the fall and the sight of his blood, causes emotional pain that can last a lifetime. The truth of his experience is that his knee was cut and he felt physical pain. While it is true that the fear may cause him to be more cautious in the future, it might also cause him to stop exploring his world with the appropriate amount of physical action necessary to keep him fit.

Many relationships are broken by our difficulty with understanding truth. Words and actions are translated into the dualistic language of emotions. Love and hate, happy and sad, and like and dislike are the words that can confuse and frustrate us. Honesty is the weapon we must use to defeat the emotions that threaten to break our relationships.

Honesty in relationships starts with confidence in our selves. If we have a poor self-image, then we will rely more upon the acceptance of others for validation of our worth. That means, a man with low self-esteem will need the constant reassurance of his partner, demonstrated as possessiveness, and sometimes, paranoia, to make him feel worthy. The man's jealousy and constant worrying about his partner leaving him is a clear sign of his emotional dependence on his partner. If the man improves his self-image, he can begin to rely less on feeding his emotional self through the relationship, and honesty can be sought and discovered within the relationship.

When an emotion comes into your heart, look for its root. If you feel anger, what was said or done to you, and how did that challenge your image of yourself? Is your anger a defensive action that your ego is taking in order to protest your self-image?

When you are embarrassed, is the root of that embarrassment a challenge to your ego that has made you question your beliefs about who and what you are? If so, then try to see how you are and accept it – this acceptance of how you are is your honesty.

"If you fall down, get up and keep going."

I ask the children to run a lot in every class. When a student is first beginning the program and he or she falls while running, they will usually look to the parent to see the parent's reaction. If they see that the parent is watching and looks worried then they cry immediately and will run to the parent. If they don't see the parent, or if the parent is not watching, then they will stand up and quickly return to running (The floors are covered with safety mats, so there is seldom any real injury that would force the child to stop).

When I see a child begin to fall, I say, "If you fall down, get up and keep running." This distracts them and directs them back to the running, avoiding any need for them to stop and experience emotional pain. If I were to go to them and show fear (a natural thing for parents to do when their child falls down), then they would learn that fear is associated with falling. After a few weeks of classes, the students have an honest understanding of the physical pain associated with falling down while running.

Chapter 10 Community

Our lives are too difficult to live by ourselves. We gain power from our relationships with our friends, family, and neighbors. We need the recognition of others to survive no matter what we might think. Even the most negative and antisocial person seeks the recognition of peers or community through his accomplishments and material possessions. No matter what he professes, deep inside he strives for acknowledgment and acceptance.

Building healthy relationships require discipline and emotional control. Communicating our needs and wants in a clear and appropriate way allows us to receive the recognition we need to be content in a relationship. Confidence, which comes from real ability and knowledge of our success, allows is to build a relationship based on true sharing.

Sharing is not giving away more than we can afford to. We must recognize that we have to take care of ourselves first in order to help others. This is not selfish, but is a guarantee that we will be able to share without jealousy or greed. A person who puts others above herself does so out of selfishness. They are trying to prove to others their goodness by suffering want. If they do not know their own goodness, then no amount of sacrifice to others will convince them of their own goodness. They will secretly harbor ill feeling toward all the people they have sacrifice for, and their relationships with them will be insincere.

Mother Theresa gave herself completely to the service of others only after providing for herself. Her relationship with God was intact and held priority above her relationship to the millions she served. She shared her love for God only after she took her fill of that love.

The Asian Arts Center

In 1998 I took over a failing commercial martial arts school as a favor for another instructor. The owner was supposed to financially support me until I could make the school profitable, but walked away shortly after turning the school over, leaving me with a stack of unpaid bills and no students.

I could have walked away when the owner did, but I am single and I like a challenge. For a few years, I have been cultivating an image of what a martial arts community should look like. I felt that in order to serve the local community, the student body should be made up of the same percentages of wealthy, middle class, and poor students as the local community.

I wanted to fill the school with students from all classes so they could meet each other and see each other's faces. The wall blocking communication among the classes has much to do with how we pass judgment on each other. We compare our experiences with what we think we know about other people. For example, we might say, "I work hard to barely make a living; I don't want to pay for someone who is too lazy to get a job." Or "shouldn't have to pay for those kids having babies. How can they bring another life into this world when they can't even feed themselves?" These comments are judgments made against a person or group based on an expectation that a common experience was shared.

I like to think this way-if you saw a baby crying because he is hungry, then you would feed him. When you think of a mother who is unable to feed her baby, instead of feeding the baby, you shake your head and say that she must not love her child enough to get off drugs and get a job. Two things are important to remember, though, if you are to save that baby. First, the baby is still hungry, regardless of your opinion of the mother. Second, you must try to see the mother in the baby (that is, the baby will grow following the mother's example, walking in the same footsteps). The model the baby learns from is flawed, not the baby.

Over time I was able to reflect the local community pretty well, and the proof of success came very quickly. We had a large group of foster children and a handful of low-income children in the program. The diverse group of parents would meet each other at the school and talk about what their children were doing tin the classes. I expected the parents to share outgrown children's clothes, and buy groceries for a needy family every once in a while. What shocked me, however, was that the parents became mentors for fellow parents.

Parents would meet at the school for their children's classes, but would walk down the mall to the café to sit and talk. They would talk about parenting, encourage a young mother to get her GED and promise to help her study. Their children had play dates with each other at the local children's museum, or the zoo. The change in the parents was dramatic and helped them reinforce the skills their children were learning.

Chapter 11 Vision

No matter how hard they try, our politicians cannot legislate morality.

The Office of National Drug Control Policy, a US government agency led by our "Drug Czar" spends hundreds of millions of dollars every year on programs that don't stop or prevent illicit drug use. Billboards, television and radio ads, magazine ads, and DARE program are well intentioned, but proven ineffective. The simple reason is that all of these approaches cannot change the behavior of their audience. It is ridiculous to say, "even if one person is saved, then it is worth it." When such incredible amounts of money is being spent.

The methods described in this book will change behavior. If you change the behavior of one child, that child will positively influence several of his peers and family members. If you teach ten children, then you affect hundreds. One hundred children affect change in an entire school. Increase the exposure to this program, and you will change society in a very short period of time. Two or three generations later, we will be conditioned to speak honestly and respectfully with each other. In twenty years, we will be working to accumulate knowledge of and experience of truth, which will soothe your souls, instead of working to accumulate material wealth and goods, which only feed our emotions.

Master Choi once told me that the problem with the parent-child relationship is that while the children are growing, the parents have stopped growing. Eventually the child will pass the parent and communication will break. Use this book to help your child to grow. That will build their faith in you. Confidence will come to you as you see the proof of your success written on your child's face. When you start challenging yourself to grow (necessary to stay ahead of your growing child), you will need the confidence that you have built to keep you going. When your confidence in yourself is not enough, then you must rely on the power of your child's faith in you. Grow with your child, and the bond between you will bring you both closer to the truth about love.

Love is intentionally left undefined in this book. I can describe what I have learned about communication, self-control, and focus, but not love. Love is at the center of truth, so you can only find love in the search for truth. When a child is born, parents often experience something much more powerful than emotion and cannot define what they are experiencing with the language of emotion. Having a child demands that you live honestly in order to find love. You won't, however, find love at the end of your quest; it is on the path you take to get there that will give you knowledge of love.

Left to right – Master Choi, Elizabeth Haley, Charlie Haley, Thiele Schroeder, Matt Pasquinilli, Kingsley Schroeder.

ABOUT THE AUTHOR

Matt Pasquinilli has been teaching martial arts to children for more than ten years. He has worked with children with physical and emotional challenges, and specializes in helping children with ADD/ADHD to control themselves without the use of mood altering medications.

In March of 2000, Mr. Pasquinilli helped found the Asian Arts Center, a 501(c)(3) non-profit corporation. The Dayton, Ohio organization provides leadership and character skills development programs to children in public and private schools. In the 2000-2001 school year, the University of Wisconsin, Madison, conducted a study on the effectiveness of the Asian Arts Center's program. In the fall of 2001, results from this study will be published in trade journals, as well as in mainstream media. Early data shows dramatic improvements in the areas of self-esteem, confidence, and focus.

To order additional copies of

The Child Whisperer

Send check to:

Asian Arts Center

27 West Whipp Rd.

Dayton, OH 45459

Quantity   Amount

_____   @$9.95 each $_____

Ohio residents please add 5% sales tax $_____

Shipping $3.00 first book $_____

                        $1.00 each additional $_____

Total amount enclosed $_____

Name   _____

Address_____

_____

www.thechildwhisperer.com

asian_arts@hotmail.com